# Experience
# **Oscar® Week:**

GET IN ON ACADEMY AWARDS® ACTION

*The Only Event Guide for
Academy Award® Fans*

BY CATHERINE R. LESTER

Experience Oscar® Week: Get in on Academy Awards® Action

The Only Event Guide for Academy Award® Fans

Written by Catherine R. Lester

ISBN: 978-0-578-44201-3 paperback

Library of Congress Control Number 2019900014

Copyright 2019 - Catherine R. Lester

Cover Design by rebecacovers

Edited by Lydia K. Ingram

Author portrait by Tammy Lechner

Revised Edition 2023

Publisher: Company Voice Box LLC.

# TABLE OF CONTENTS

# DEDICATION

*To my husband, Cray*
*Thank you for loving me just the way I am and holding*
*down the fort while I run away from home to attend Oscar Week.*

# INTRODUCTION

I t's safe to say, if you're reading this guide, you enjoy watching the Academy Awards. I'd bet the two of us could spend hours talking about Oscar-nominated films we've seen, or we could chat about previous award programs because we're really into the pomp and circumstance of it all. What I want to do for you is to enhance your Academy Award experience exponentially. This guide, which is based on my own research and experience, will reveal how you can be smack dab in the middle of the grandeur of official Academy of Motion Picture Arts and Sciences (AMPAS) film events, without special connections, and for next to nothing.

## AND YOU ARE ...?

I'm an entertainment industry outsider who has discovered the inside scoop to golden opportunities that most fans don't know exist. My fan experience includes viewing every Academy Awards best picture nominee since 1997 and attending AMPAS public events: Oscar Week, Oscar Red Carpet Fan Experience, Oscar Concert, Oscar Night at the Museum, and the grand opening of the Academy Museum of Motion Pictures in Los Angeles, and Oscar Roadtrip and Oscar Fan Experience in Texas. I'm also a founding donor of the Academy Museum of Motion Pictures.

Like most Academy Award fans, I love to watch the nominated films before, during, and after the Oscars.

Unlike most viewers, I delve into the majority of what is being offered to fans by the Academy, ranging from silly video contests to traveling halfway across Texas to hold an Oscar statuette. During awards season, I read industry publications, review analysts' reports, document fan engagement activities, cheer nominees on social media, and watch related TV programs. As an Oscar fanatic, it's what I do.

## TENURED AFICIONADO

Before I became an Academy Award diehard, I had been tuning in, off and on, for decades to get a glimpse of my favorite actors and actresses. I transitioned from fan to aficionado in 1997 when *The English Patient* (1996) was nominated for best picture. I wasn't familiar with the top talent in the movie, but I loved the film. It was the combination of Ralph Fiennes' sweet eyes, the exotic desert location, the sinful deeds of a married woman, and the magnetic attraction the main characters had for each other that did it for me. I was intrigued and curious to know what other movies had been nominated for best picture, so when I reviewed the list of all the nominees and discovered there were only a couple I had not yet seen that year, I decided to see all of them so that I could make an informed decision about which film was most deserving of an Academy Award. My appreciation for film as an art was sparked, and my cultural journey officially began.

Since 1997, I've seen every movie nominated for best picture, for very good reasons. First, I take it as a cultural arts challenge because I'm willing to see movies that aren't typically my favorite genre. It sounds like an easy task, but quite frankly there have been some nominated movies I didn't want to see; films about hobbits, foreign conflicts, teen oppression, and slavery are not usually what I pay to see. Get me now? How authentic is a cultural journey if you stay with what is familiar? Also, I want to judge the nominees fairly to predict a winner. Although I don't have an official Oscar vote, I can certainly see for myself if the small independent film is deserving of accolades or if the big-budget movie was worse than promised. Besides, once I had viewed five years in a row, I had to uphold my reputation of consecutive annual viewing of best picture nominees, and I'm pleased as punch to have surpassed the 25-year mark.

While on this journey, I have made an effort to look at movies from less popular categories, such as short films, documentaries, animated movies, and foreign language films. In previous award seasons, animated and foreign language movies have shown up on the best picture nomination list, and on occasion, I have seen the short film categories. Nowadays, the short films are easier to view because they're presented in a series. It is sometimes more difficult to view documentaries and foreign language movies, as they often have limited distribution; but where there's a will, there's a way. Sometimes after awards season, I'd get DVDs of the nominated documentaries and foreign language movies from my local library, then view them at my leisure, instead of trying to cram in viewings before the big night.

Although I've seen a lot of nominated films, I'm not an encyclopedia of Oscar history. I'm pretty good at remembering the award winners for the best picture category, but beyond that, I can't remember the hosts for previous awards ceremonies or statistics about the nomination-to-award ratio for repeat nominees. I can, however, tell you about the different ways to win bleacher seats that have been offered to fans in the past few years because I tried practically all of them!

## OSCAR ENGAGEMENT

Back in the day, the Academy of Motion Picture Arts and Sciences partnered with nonprofit organizations across the United States, allowing them to host sanctioned Oscar parties, known as The Oscar Experience, as a fundraiser. A patron's ticket purchase included admission to a viewing event, an official Oscar program—the same one Academy Award attendees receive—and an Oscar poster, among other things. I attended these while they lasted because it was really cool to be a part of an official Oscar event, and the event trinkets were great keepsakes for my memory box.

The only other time I know of the Academy intentionally reaching into other cities was its Oscar Roadshow in 2013, when two hosts and a crew traveled to select U.S. cities to give fans an opportunity to behold an Oscar statuette. Lucky for me, they made a stop in Texas, so I hit the highway and visited all the locations on their itinerary on the day the team was in Houston. Although I wasn't one of the fortunate folks who won bleacher seats being given to adoring fans selected at random, I did score several shots with the little gold knight.

Other than that, most of the outreach to fans outside of Los Angeles has been on social media. Fans are called to action all the time, but offering followers the opportunity to connect usually happens during awards season.

To be fair about the Academy's outreach, they do provide a variety of screenings and such year-round at their venues in Los Angeles and sometimes New York—that's great for residents in those areas. I also know they've supported film festivals in other cities.

## SO WHAT?

I'm sharing all of this because there exists a grand opportunity that very few people know about: the opportunity to experience the magic and splendor of the Academy Awards through Oscar Week events in Los Angeles. Academy Award friends and followers who really get into it—those who, like me, view nominated films and tune in to the program year after year—deserve to know that they, too, can attend official AMPAS events leading up to the big night.

Sharing knowledge is what makes the world go around, so it's my privilege to reveal the inside scoop.

Oscar Week 2016 was a milestone in my life, and I'm sure a future Oscar Week could be a high point in your life, too. My goal for writing this book is to educate you about Oscar Week, instruct you on how to engage, inform you about film art resources, and amplify your Academy Award experience.

# PART I:

# OSCAR WEEK

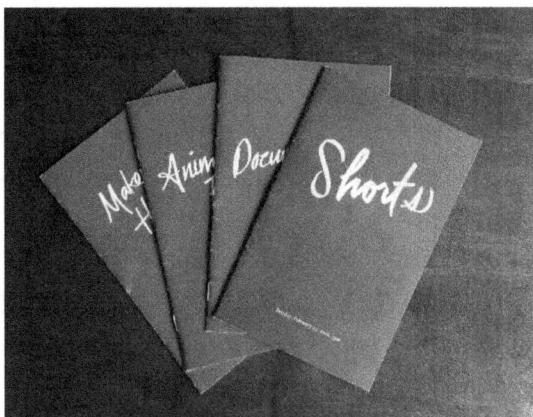

# CHAPTER 1-

## Showcasing Motion Picture Excellence

Of all the ceremonies that honor excellence in film, the annual Academy Awards are at the top of the heap, year after year. From the time the nominees are announced, movie fans all over the globe join in the thrill and excitement of it all. With the media reporting everything from designer gowns to after-party plans, people are watching and reading about all of the pomp and circumstance that happens days and weeks before the golden statuette takes the stage on Oscar Night.

But unbeknownst to most fans outside of the Hollywood Hills, there is a special, almost-secret event that precedes Tinsel Town's biggest night of the year: Oscar Week. Hosted by the Academy of Motion Picture Arts and Sciences (AMPAS), Oscar Week is a series of individual events celebrating select categories. The Oscar-nominated films are featured by category, and the events highlight filmmakers in question-and-answer-style panel discussions. It's a stellar event that is mainly publicized within AMPAS's social media and its A.Frame digital magazine and Academy Museum of Motion Pictures member newsletters and social media. Hardcore fans who really stay connected to AMPAS activities and events know about Oscar Week through these channels.

# OSCAR WEEK

## What Oscar Week Is

Oscar Week is a series of public programs in the days that precede the Oscars in which filmmakers participate in a panel discussion about their films that have been nominated for an Academy Award. The week has five or six individual events, each dedicated to a specific Oscar award category.

The purpose of Oscar Week is to celebrate select categories of nominated films, but it's more than that. Not only is it an opportunity to educate the public about excellence in filmmaking, but it also introduces audience members to different cultures. It's inspiring to hear the ups and downs filmmakers experienced through their movie-making process. You are in the same room with Oscar nominees, and hearing their stories of trials and triumphs during the filmmaking process is both thrilling and inspiring. It makes you feel connected to the filmmakers and their movies on a deeper level.

Most of the films honored during Oscar Week are not typical mainstream movies. The select categories are:

Animated Short and Feature Films
Documentary Short and Feature Films
Live Action Short and International Feature Films
Makeup and Hairstyling

Just recently, AMPAS began hosting Oscars Night at the Museum, a 7-hour Academy Awards viewing party for movie fans at the Academy Museum of Motion Pictures. It's a new addition to Oscar Week and its format is vastly different than the other week's events. It has all of the glamorous elements you'd expect from an Academy Awards party in Los Angeles, and the perfect event for cinephiles who want to dress up for this glitzy movie event of the year.

On occasion, there is an Oscar Concert. This musical event seldom occurs, and although it's part of Oscar Week, it's not promoted with the other events.

All of the events for the week, except the Oscar Concert, take place at the Academy Museum of Motion Pictures. Prior to the museum's opening, Oscar Week took place at the Samuel Goldwyn Theater, which is located in the same building as the Academy of Motion Picture Arts and Sciences' headquarters, 8949 Wilshire Boulevard, Beverly Hills, California, 90211. Oscar Week events are spread out throughout the day, with a least one evening event per day, and all take place in the David Geffen theater located inside the museum's sphere, an architectural wonder. The theater is a one of a kind cinema space featuring plush seats and crisp sound quality to provide an exceptional movie-viewing experience.

The program for the individual events listed above differs slightly. Some screen full films, though a majority of them show trailers or film clips. A few have movie posters and movie props on display; some have actors and crew in attendance. The duration of each event varies as well, ranging from one and a half to three hours in length.

## History

These events were rolled out individually over the years as independent programs, but they were eventually consolidated to create Oscar Week, officially named in 2014. The first category showcased was foreign language in the 1950s, and the events were actually press conferences. In terms of honoring foreign language films for an Oscar, the Academy recognized foreign language films with special awards beginning in 1947. Then in 1956, the Academy officially created the foreign language film category, and later renamed it the international feature film category in 2019.

In the early 1980s, short film programming made its debut and took place after the Oscars. Short films officially became an Oscar category for the 5th Academy Awards in 1931–1932, officially named short subjects, and this category included cartoons, comedies, and novelties. The films referred to as comedies and novelties prompted the creation of the live action category in 1957 for the 30th Oscars.

The makeup and hairstylist symposium began in 2007. In the 1960s, AMPAS recognized only makeup artists and awarded special recognition for their outstanding work. In 1981, a makeup category was created for the 54th Academy Awards, thereafter granting Oscar statuettes to winners. Hairstyling was added to this category in 2012, and beginning with the 85th Oscars, the category was renamed makeup and hairstyling.

The animated feature program was added in 2009. For decades, and since the beginning of the Academy Awards in the 1930s, animated films were referred to as cartoons. Because they were short in length, cartoons were considered short films. It was in 2001 for the 74th Academy Awards when feature-length animated films were recognized as a category.

The documentaries program started in 2010. Documentaries, feature-length, and shorts have been a part of Oscar history since 1941, when they were sanctioned for the 16th Academy Awards.

Oscars Night at the Museum was added in 2022, just as the world was beginning to recover from the Corona virus pandemic. The opening of the Academy Museum of Motion Pictures in 2021 enabled AMPAS to use its space to invite Academy Award fans to a viewing party in 2022. The museum has a 900+ seat theater and food dining areas, thus making an enormous space to entertain movie fans.

## What Oscar Week Isn't

Oscar Week is artistically inspiring in a dignified way. You're not going to find screaming fans, celebrities on a red carpet, or lights and photographers, like you would on Oscar night. If you're planning to attend just to get a glimpse of a famous actor, actress, or nominee, you'll be disappointed. When you approach the venue, you might even question if you're at the right place because it looks like a typical day at the museum.

The event series is a quiet and reserved type of excitement, perhaps because the focus is art, not celebrity. If you do Oscar Week right (see Chapter 2 Exceptional Experience), you will push your cultural boundaries farther than you ever have in your life, and you will no doubt be inspired. If you're looking for something to help you move the needle on your creative scale, this is it. Don't be surprised if you walk away with an idea for a killer movie or plot points for a screenplay before the week is over. The impact these events have on creative types is huge.

Although it is called Oscar *Week*, it is not actually a full week of events. The individual events take place over the course of four days. The name Oscar Week merely indicates that these sanctioned events take place the week prior to the Academy Awards.

## Who Attends Oscar Week?

The great thing about Oscar Week is that tickets are available to the public. Ordinary folks with absolutely no Hollywood connections can purchase a ticket to any or all of the individual events. Chapter 2 Exceptional Experience has ticket information.

Those who are fascinated by film production, back stories, and the diversity of film genres will thoroughly enjoy Oscar Week events. The panel discussions focus on film as an art form, so the majority of audience members are either in the business or are fans of a particular genre.

Attendees in the room include AMPAS members, former Academy Award nominees and winners, film industry professionals, film students, film fans, and of course, the directors, producers, and perhaps some cast and crew from the films being featured at each event. Basically, the crowd looks like ordinary people, so if you were standing next to an Oscar winner in the international feature film category or short live action category, you might not even know it because there is nothing flashy or stereotypically celebrity about them. Audience members can range in age from 20 to 60 and beyond.

The following chapters include details for planning a tremendous trip. It's never too early to start checking out the landscape. Your itinerary can be simple or complex, but the most important thing is to be an early bird. Allow yourself plenty of time to eat beforehand and find parking so you can get to the Academy Museum of Motion

Pictures for the main event with time to spare. Get the most bang for your buck and stay the entire day to enjoy all there is being offered for the single price of admission per day.

## OSCAR WEEK EVENTS

### Day One: Animated Short Films and Animated Feature Films

This is the most popular event of the week, and the house is packed. Oscar Week begins on the Wednesday before the Academy Awards ceremony with the animated feature film and short film category.. The day's program schedule is:

11 a.m. Animated short films screening

1 p.m. Panel of animated short film nominees

3 p.m. Animated short films screening (encore)

6 p.m. Panel of animated feature film nominees

Each session kicks off with a brief welcome message from staff member of the Academy Museum and an Academy governor. In the past, Jon Bloom, the Academy governor representing the short films and feature animation branch of AMPAS, addressed the audience. Then Jennifer Yuh Nelson, filmmaker of the Oscar-nominated animated feature *Kung Fu Panda* (2008), took it from there. The introductions are highly information, as they relay statistics about that year's competition and insight into the selection of the final nominees.

All of the short films are screened at the 11 a.m. session, then an encore at 3 p.m. the same day. There are five nominees for the animated short film category, and all are required to be less than 40 minutes in length. Most are from producers and directors outside the United States, so the movies are unique and different from what most American audiences are used to. They are often extremely creative and exceptionally well done.

At the 1 p.m. session animated short filmmakers participate in a question and at the 6 p.m. session the animated feature filmmakers participate in a panel discussion. This is when the audience gets to sit in on in-depth discussions about the unique movie-making process from the technical and creative side.

The presentation format is the same. A governor from the short films and feature animation branch officially welcomes the audience before handing the microphone over to animated filmmakers who facilitate the Q&As. The Academy members who host and moderate are highly accomplished in their field and have been an Oscar nominee in the past.

Sometimes the nominees are foreign language animated films, which contributes to a diversity in film styles. For those studying animation, this is a great category, as it analyzes filmmaking from a technical perspective, including style and method. Interestingly, the content of some of these films is intended for adults and is not subject matter for children. Being that this event is about film as art, the plots aren't necessarily about rainbows and butterflies but real-life situations.

## Day Two: Documentary Short and Feature Films

The Thursday before the Oscars is designated for documentaries. The filmmakers who produce these movies are motivated by human nature and seek to reveal humanity in its raw environment. Common knowledge among industry professionals is that documentarians don't do it for the money. The day's program schedule is:

11 a.m. Documentary short films screening

1 p.m. Panel of documentary short film nominees

3 p.m. Documentary short films screening (encore)

6 p.m. Panel of documentary feature film nominees

Following suit to the day before, typically an Academy member who is a documentary branch governor introduces the short subject program, and another will moderate the feature documentary program. The documentary short subject films are screened first, then those filmmakers participate in a panel discussion. Thereafter, the documentary feature filmmakers gather for a panel discussion in the same format.

The talent and creativity these filmmakers bring to the table are diverse. Nominees for the Academy Awards in this category include previous Oscar nominees and first-time documentarians. Instead of actors, these films may include illustrations or compilations of archived video clips.

These sessions are fascinating because the audience learns how the filmmakers came across their subjects and what motivated them to capture the story. For some, the subject matter is an element of their culture they deemed morally wrong. Others witnessed human triumph in devastating situations. The topics range from removing Ebola-stricken dead bodies in Liberia to biographies about troubled, famous female vocalists. These sessions unveil numerous dimensions about filmmaking and the subjects of the movie that are entertaining and educational, making for an enriching experience for cinephiles.

## Day Four: Live Action Short Films and International Feature Films

Most of the producers and directors are from outside the United States, so the movies in these categories are unique and different from what most American audiences are used to. They are often extremely creative and exceptionally well done. The day's program schedule is:

11 a.m. Live action short films screening

1 p.m. Panel of live action short film nominees

3 p.m. Live action short films screening (encore)

6 p.m. Panel of international feature film nominees

This category really pushes filmgoers to expand their boundaries culturally and to broaden their perspective of film as an art. Foreign language films take American audiences out of their comfort zone because the movies are in languages that may be strange to them, and the stories take place in a part of the world they may not be familiar with. Although the language, dress, and customs are different than you might be used to, there is one element that is the same for all: humanity. These films are about life, tragedy, and triumph. You either discover or are reminded we're all the same—no matter what language we speak or where we're from, people around the world deal with many of the same issues. Foreign language films prove that the human experience transcends cultural differences.

The international feature film category has been a hot topic in recent years because those films are have deemed worthy of a best picture nomination. In 2023, *All Quiet on the Western Front* (2022), in 2022, *Drive My Car* (2021), and in 2020 *Parasite* (2019), which received the Academy Award for best picture and best international feature films. There is more to the category than subtitles, so be sure get the filmmakers' point of view about their work at this panel discussion.

## Day Four: Makeup and Hairstyling Symposium

This event, the finale of Oscar Week panel-styled showcases, takes place Saturday afternoon and is one of the most popular because there is a lot of show and tell. In addition to the movie clips and Q&A portion, there is an exhibit of facial molds, hair pieces, and design tools demonstrating the work that goes into the physical creation of the movie characters. The schedule is:

1 p.m. Panel of makeup and hairstyling nominees

3 p.m. Exhibit of nominees' work

The category was established in 1981, and current rules stipulate that no more than five films can be nominated for this category. Nominated artists take the stage, one film at a time, to answer questions about their work. After this one-by-one team dialogue concludes, the audience proceeds to the symposium to see the artists work on display.

Makeup and hairstyling helps define movie characters. In some cases, it's used to age a character, and in other cases, it's used to reveal wounds that are a part of the character's past or present.

The artists share their process, ranging from researching the proper materials in which to design and create the look desired by the director, to issues they encountered on the set. On occasion, the actors are in attendance too, so audiences get a better understanding of the craftsmanship involved in creating their characters.

When the Q&A concludes, the sublevel of the museum's lobby displays a variety of makeup and hairstyling elements from the nominated films. There are photographs of the artists in action as well as facial and body appliques that were used to transform the actors into the film's characters. The displays allow the audience to understand the characters more deeply and to learn how a second skin is designed, developed, and applied to the actors in those roles.

## Oscar Concert

This musical event is an official Academy Award event that is promoted separately from Oscar Week. This one-off event, which seldom occurs, honors the nominees for best original score and original song in a concert which occurs during Oscar Week. The composers for each best original score stand before a full orchestra and conduct them to play the theme music from the nominated film. It's an exceptional experience to hear the music from a live orchestra and to feel how the music elicits the mood of the film's thematic tone. In most cases, the featured composers have accomplished notable work for numerous other films, and seeing these legends in action is unforgettable.

As of this writing, the event has only occurred twice. In 2014, it took place at UCLA's Royce Hall, and in 2018, it was at the Walt Disney Concert Hall in Los Angeles. The program does not follow a particular format, nor does it incorporate the Q&A elements of the other Oscar Week events. Both times the concert has taken place, it occurred the same night as another Oscar Week event; so if you attend the concert, you'll most likely be missing out on another Oscar Week event.

## Oscars Night at the Museum

The ultimate movie fan experience is attending the official Academy Awards viewing party hosted by AMPAS at the Academy Museum of Motion Pictures. Giving Oscar fans the opportunity to party at a sanctioned event at an AMPAS venue is long overdue, and this open invitation to the public is gracious especially since the actual Academy Awards ceremony is exclusive.

This is the night for Academy Awards fans to get dressed up to look and feel like the star they are to bask in the glory of all things Oscar. All areas of the museum are open, including spaces typically reserved for private events for AMPAS members. The interior and exterior are decorated beautifully and elegantly, staying true to the stature, high class and prominence of the Academy Awards. The schedule is:

3 p.m. Red carpet opens, beverage service opens, DJ in piazza

4 p.m. Oscars preshow telecast begins in theater, buffet dinner is served

5 p.m. Oscars ceremony telecast begin

8 p.m. After-party begins

The excitement and energy at this party raise the roof because the collective enthusiasm for being in Oscar's house for this one-night-only special event is phenomenal, and a dream come true for many in attendance. Patrons range from film fans to industry professionals. You'll see journalists and social media influencers reporting live, movie fans wearing decorative items from their favorite nominees, talent and crew from nominated films, and museum staff dressed creatively for the big night. Go solo or take friends with you. Either way, this event is a must-do.

# CHAPTER 2 -

# Exceptional Experience

The magic of Oscar Week is proper preparation, so these areemty important things you need to know about making this an exceptional experience. This information, which pertains to all Oscar Week events except the Oscar Concert, will help you get off to a good start, and you'll look like an experienced attendee because you'll have the inside scoop.

## PLANNING

### Mark Your Calendar

Getting a jump start on Oscar Week requires planning. The great news is that you already know it happens the same week as the Academy Awards, so all you have to do is find out the date for the Oscars.

Typically, AMPAS announces key dates for the next Oscar season during the summer. Important dates include the day of the next Academy Awards, the date the nominations are announced, start and end dates for voting members, and the date for the Scientific and Technical Awards. Unfortunately, Oscar Week is not on the list of key dates, but at least you know it's typically the Wednesday through Saturday before the big night.

Go to www.oscars.org to find this information. Click News, then click News and Updates. Scroll until you find a title that relays key dates. Even though Oscar Week is not listed in the key dates announcement, count on the schedule this is outlined in Chapter 1 for animated, documentaries, live action and international feature films,: and makeup and hairstyling. Expect Oscars Night at the Museum to take place on the day of the Academy Awards ceremony. As mentioned before, the Oscar Concert is promoted separately, so do your due diligence to find out if its happening.

## Purchasing Tickets

Getting tickets to these incredible events is really easy and all screening and panel events are shockingly nominal; however, when the ticket sales begin, the seats sell out very quickly. The early bird scores, and the secret to securing seats is knowing when ticket sales open.

The best way to score tickets to the Oscar Week screenings, panel discussions and Oscars Night at the Museum is by being a member of the Academy Museum because members get first notice of Oscar Week ticket sales. To be a museum member, you must purchase a membership package and there are many options. The best option is to purchase a $190 dual museum member that provides privileges for you and one companion. If you plan on you and a friend attending Oscar Week events together, this is the way to go. If you're a solo act, then a $100 individual membership is the way to go.

Solidify your membership purchase as soon as possible, and no later than 2 months before the Oscars so that you are included in the museum's announcements about tickets for Oscar Week events. Members are informed before the general public is aware of ticket sales, and members get pre-sale privileges, essentially guaranteeing seats.

On the surface it seems counter intuitive to buy a museum membership to then get Oscar Week event tickets but it's an investment that pays off in the long run even though at first glance it seems like you're paying just to get a discount. The most valuable benefit to purchasing a museum membership is that daily admission to the Academy Museum is free, including admission to Oscar Week events. The Oscars Night at the Museum is the only exception due to the nature of the event. To be clear, your museum membership grants you free admission to the Oscar Week events outlined in Chapter 1 for animated, documentaries, live action and international feature films, and makeup and hairstyling. In addition, members get expedited check-in and priority seating at these events. Even though there is no cost to members, tickets are still required for admission, and its easy to secure tickets online during the member pre-sale period.

Typically, the Academy Museum of Motion Pictures begins online ticket sales to the general public the first week of the month that precedes the Academy Awards. For example if the Oscars are in March, ticket sales for Oscar Week and Oscar Night at the Museum begin in February. If you forego the museum membership for perks, keep an eye on the museum's events calendar and their social media feeds. If you don't see it, that means tickets are not yet available, so revisit another time.

The museum controls all of the ticket sales, so going through a ticket broker is not an option. Once online sales are active, you can purchase directly from their website. The $25 price per day of admission for an adult includes admission to Oscar Week events, expect Oscars Night but be sure to select the Oscar Week ticket when purchasing. Fun fact: Prior to the museum's opening, AMPAS hosted Oscar Week at their headquarters in Beverly Hills and the cost per ticket was $5 per person, per session for the short film, documentaries, animated features, and international films events. The makeup and hairstyling symposium was free of charge. Yes, you read correctly. Five dollars-to-free of charge.

Oscars Night at the Museum admission tickets are handled slightly differently. Members have to pay to attend this party; it is not included as a membership benefit. The opportunity to purchase Oscars Night tickets in a pre-sale is the perk and members are limited to the quantity of their membership level. For example, an individual member is limited to one pre-sale ticket purchase and a dual membership is limited to two pre-sale tickets. When ticket sales are open to the general public, members may purchase more. In 2023, tickets were $250 per person and in 2022, tickets were $100 per person, so be aware there might be a price hike for future events.

Tickets to the Oscar Concert are processed differently. Tickets are available months in advance and are processed through the concert venue or the ticket agent. Although this event does occur during Oscar Week, it's promoted separately, so be diligent in your search for event information. Admission typically starts at $50.

## PATRON PROTOCOL

The David Geffen theater inside the mystical elevated glass sphere at the Academy Museum of Motion Pictures is a venue of simple elegance where dignified aficionados of motion pictures are enriched artistically and culturally. It's not a venue for screaming fans and raving patrons. To keep things orderly and decorous, there are a few things you should know before walking through the door.

### Security Check

For the safety of all involved, patrons are required to pass through a metal detector at the museum's entrance. Handbags are also opened and checked, so remove your unmentionables beforehand. Leave your pocket knives, mace and scissors in the car.

## Food and Beverage

There are no concession stands because food and drink are prohibited. Don't even think of stashing snacks in your bag because you'll get snagged at the security check. Eat a big meal before showtime. Bottled water is permissible.

If you're attending a couple of session in a single day, you can grab some grub in between sessions at Fanny's. There is also an outdoor café within walking distance at LACMA. If possible, map out some other dining options in advance since you'll be pressed for time and will want to dine within walking distance.

## Autographs

When each Q&A concludes, nominees on the stage may be rushed by fans asking for autographs. Sometimes there is an announcement beforehand prohibiting autographs, so this is a hit or miss. Know that when the Q&As are finished, the nominees are usually crowded by their own entourage, so wading through the mass of people is a bit cumbersome. The best option is to dash down to the museum's entrance to get a better glimpse of nominees as they exit the building.

# Q&As

All of the question and answer sessions are facilitated by the moderator. Most of the individual events aren't like typical film festivals where the filmmakers take questions from the audience after the screening. Attendees at the makeup and hairstyling event may be invited to ask questions at the end of the program. Other than that, if you have a burning question, your best bet is to tweet it.

## Exit Quickly

When each event concludes, theater staff encourage your immediate departure, but folks linger to get a closer look at the nominees, or they wait their turn to take a picture in front of the Oscar statuettes. Staff are persistent, so be nimble when the event ends.

## Merchandise

The museum's store has a lot to offer. Merchandise ranges from $5 magnets to $700 chairs. Most of the items are limited editions, meaning once they sell out, that's it. Therefore, buy multiples of the items you really love because they won't be available in the future. Museum members get a discount for purchases at the store, and for those on a $0 budget, the wristbands used for Oscar Week admission is a fun keepsake.

## Event Programs

In years past, ticket holders use to get a beautifully designed and informative program for each individual event that made for wonderful souvenirs. These programs would include the names of AMPAS members, board of governors, moderators and nominees names but now it's a slide show with only the Oscar Week schedule. Take something to write with when in attendance to catch all the names and positions of the AMPAS members and nominees participating in Oscar Week panels.

## Photography

Patrons may take pictures before and after but not during the event. AMPAS films the event and owns the copyright to the live content. Their video is posted on YouTube a few days or weeks after the event. Folks who take photos during the event are immediately approached by theater staff reminding them no photography is allowed. Know that theater staff are relentless about this and there are no special privileges for VIPS. That rule applies to everyone.

Pictures are allowed by the Oscar statuette located inside the David Geffen theater, and its best to do so before the session begins. Know that the lighting is bad, so there is no point in trying multiple angles to get a perfect shot. What you get is as good as it gets, so just take the picture and move on. The Oscar statuette is moved to another location after the session concludes, so waiting until the end is a bad option.

## Seating

Even though seating is a first come, first serve situation, there is reserved seating for museum members, AMPAS members and nominees' guests at the David Geffen theater. The reserved seats are marked, some with a gold banner and some with a black banner, typically towards the front of the stage for screenings and panel discussions. On Oscars Night, it's a free for all

It's better to be early than late, so plan accordingly. Typically, the theater opens 30 minutes before each screenings and panel discussions. There is a set time for the theater's opening on Oscars Night at the Museum on the evening of the Academy Awards. If the 900+ seat theater fills to capacity, then people must leave before letting more in. Since the screening and panel sessions are more time-block based, patrons typically stay for the entire session whereas on Oscars Night, people go in and out of the theater as the evening progresses

## Attire

Your wardrobe for the screenings and panels is a different style than on the evening of the Academy Awards. No matter which event you're attending, first and foremost, wear something comfortable, particularly your shoes because there is a lot of walking. Folks attending the screenings and panels wear everything from coordinating tie-dye shirts and pants to formal dress. For the sessions preceding Oscars Night, you can pretty much wear whatever you like. Keep in mind, you are in an iconic venue, so dress the part. It's not a bad idea to at least wear business casual attire. Remember, industry professionals are there, and you never know who you're going to meet. It's also a good idea to pack a sweater or wear a long-sleeved jacket because it can get cold inside the theater.

Formal attire is best for attending Oscars Night at the Museum. You'll look smashing in your outfit, walking the red carpet and will feel like the star that you are in the company of others who are dressed to the hilt. There is a lot of walking and most of the time you'll be standing to take advantage of all of the activities offered that night. Since there is a coat check, take a comfy pair of shoes and check them in upon arrival, then change into them for the after party so you can dance the night away.

## Parking

There are parking garages very close to the museum that are better options than street parking. Public parking is available at the LA County Museum of Arts' Pritzker covered parking garage off of 6th street, a great option especially if it's raining. The next closest is at the Petersen Automotive Museum off of Fairfax, which is a short walk across a busy intersection. Smaller parking lots are adjacent, some covered, some not.

Rideshare is another option and the drop off spot is off of Fairfax at Orange. There is a drive way on Fairfax for rideshare to drive through mapped as Roddenberry Ln, Los Angeles, CA 90036. It is safe to depart the vehicle there however, traffic is typically very heavy so it may take a while for the area to clear so the rideshare driver can pull in. The entrance to the museum's grounds is at the same location, so there might also be a great deal of pedestrian traffic. This is especially true if taking rideshare for Oscars Night; you might spend more time sitting in traffic because about 2,000 people are headed to the same party at the same time.

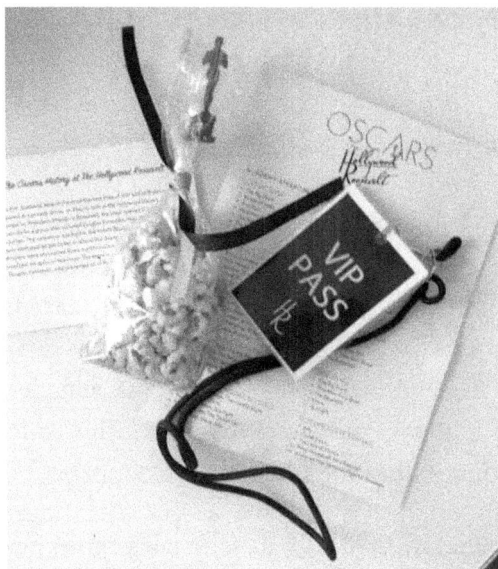

# CHAPTER 3 -

## Building Momentum

A nticipation is the fuel that flames the passion of Academy Award fans, and there are a variety of fun and exciting activities you can do to set that blaze afire months and weeks ahead of Oscar Week. These recommendations are not a be-all, do-all list; however, they're a great starting point. Whether you consume a little bit of content or a lot, excitement will build as you prepare for the most exciting week-long film event of your life.

# SPARK EXCITEMENT EARLY ON

## 3–5 Months Prior

*Track Down Nominee Shortlists*

In early fall, AMPAS announces international feature films and feature documentaries that qualify for an Academy Award. A list of these films is released, typically in October, to give film art fans a hint of what's to come. The list for international feature films includes country name, film name, and director's name. The list for feature documentaries has the film names in alphabetical order.

In late fall, AMPAS disseminates more news about international feature films and feature documentaries, and it spotlights short documentaries, animated features, live action short films, and animated short films. The organization cascades information about these categories typically in December, narrowing down the number of films being evaluated as Oscar-worthy. The shortlist includes approximately 10 international feature language films, 15 documentaries, 10 short documentaries, 10 short live-action films, and 10 animated short films. AMPAS members of each respective branch will then determine the final five films for an Academy Award nomination. Preliminary voting for the animated feature film category and international feature film category is open to all eligible voting members; it's not limited to the branch members of that category.

In addition, the songs that qualify for best original song and the musical scores that qualify for best original score are released in the late fall. For an original song to be eligible, it must be from a feature-length motion picture and consist of original words. It must also have been specifically written for the film. The music must be used in the body of the film or as the first music cue in the end credits. Academy members from the music branch receive movie clips and vote for up to five nominees, in order of preference. A maximum of two songs from any one film can be nominated. In regard to best original score, only music branch members can nominate up to five composers. Each score must be by only one composer, however there are exceptions for two equal collaborators. The score must be original and written specifically for a feature film, and must comprise of 35 percent of total music in the movie.

Nominees for makeup and hairstyling are also shortlisted in late fall. At least ten films are listed, and members of the makeup and hairstyling branch watch 10-minute video clips from each film, then nominate five films for an Academy Award.

*Subscribe to The Hollywood Reporter*

Several months before the Academy Awards, tap into the pre-nomination buzz by subscribing to The Hollywood Reporter (THR), a weekly industry magazine. The publication has articles from top-notch award analysts, feature stories about potential nominees, results from other prominent award programs and film festivals around the world, and of course, profile pieces about the hot ticket talent starring in the movies we're rooting for, and not.

I highly recommend Oscar diehards subscribe. I learned quite a bit about the Academy Award process, how studios promote their films, how favoritism begins at preceding film festivals, and what conflicts and issues exist within the industry. THR has published Q&A transcripts from anonymous Academy members who revealed their voting preferences and why. In addition, each issue is loaded with tons of fun and fascinating information leading up to the Academy Awards—everything from a revealing list of pre-Oscar parties to fashion trends on awards night.

THR is available in print and online. A digital subscription is available immediately and is delivered to your inbox much faster than the mail delivery of the print 10"x13" version. The magazine publishes a special Oscar issue, which can be a great keepsake if you order the print edition.

One of THR's outstanding team members is Scott Feinberg, executive editor of awards who reviews and evaluates Broadway shows, television programs, and motion pictures for the Tony Awards, the Emmy Awards, and the Academy Awards and then some. He has a wealth of knowledge regarding all of these art forms, and he eloquently shares his take on the projected winners.

In regard to film, Feinberg has a mighty fine podcast called Awards Chatter, which is a marvelous complement to the profile stories featured in the magazine. Being an

Oscar fanatic, Feinberg interviews industry gurus such as J.J. Abrams and Meryl Streep, asking questions about current projects and probing for answers about the upcoming Oscar season. He is a gracious host, and he brings out the best in his guests, giving listeners insight into the guest's craft, revealing their feelings about co-workers, and eliciting their thoughts about the Academy Awards.

In addition, during movie award season, Feinberg maintains an active blog on THR's website called The Race. Being exceptionally skilled in forecasting award winners—a talent he's utilized for more than 15 years—Feinberg publishes his predictions for every category before and after the Oscar nominations, even up to a day before the big night.

## 1–2 Months Prior

*Save Nominee List*

On the day the nominees are announced, AMPAS has a complete list of the nominees beautifully formatted in a PDF that is available for download from the ABC-TV's website. Saving this list is very helpful when determining which movies you need to see, remembering the categories for Oscar Week, and helping you mark your vote for the film you predict as a winner. The nominees are announced weeks before Oscar Week tickets go on sale, so use it as your movie viewing checklist and get a head start on seeing the nominees that will be featured during Oscar Week.

*View Nominated Films*

For an optimal Oscar Week experience, see all of the films beforehand for the programs you're attending. The only exception are the short films: animation, documentary and live action categories because those are shown at the Oscar Week event sessions. Seeing the entire feature films spot lit at Oscar Week gives you a heightened perspective about the character's journey, the type of environmental conditions the filmmaker is dealing with, and the approach the filmmaker took to capture the story. There are plenty of movie theaters in Los Angeles that screen these films, so don't sweat it if these nominated films don't make it to your town; you can see them while you're in L.A.

When you've spent nearly two hours or longer watching a motion picture, you develop a connection with the movie characters. Such a connection is unlikely to form if you only see a two-minute excerpt of the film. When you've seen the entire film, you know exactly what the filmmakers are referencing in the Q&As, so you're better able to relate to them, and you get more out of the Oscar Week experience.

*Watch "And the Oscar Goes To"*

The history lesson relayed in this documentary gives viewers the inside scoop about the Academy Awards' early beginnings, a peek at some of the turbulent times, the backstory from former hosts, and commentary from individuals who won and others who walked home empty-handed. This official AMPAS film is very entertaining and highly educational, so make it a permanent part of your annual prep work.

*Read 85 Years of the Oscar*

This 472-page book, written by Robert Osborne, is officially sanctioned by AMPAS. It contains colorful and sometimes shocking stories relaying decades of Oscar history. Osborne, who is best known for hosting Turner Classic Movies (TCM), was a journalist for The Hollywood Reporter for more than two decades, and he's an expert on film history. Oscar fans will be delighted by what they read and see— nominees are listed per award year, and there are more than 750 photographs in this 2-inch-thick hefty hardcover book.

*Listen to Podcast*

Behind the Screen podcast is hosted by Carolyn Giardina, tech editor for The Hollywood Reporter. She interviews industry professionals, such as composers, editors, and cinematographers about their work, giving listeners insight to technical aspects of filmmaking.

## 1–4 Weeks Prior

*Follow A.M.P.A.S. and the Academy Museum of Motion Pictures*

On occasion, the Academy hosts contests on its social media platforms, giving fans a chance to win prizes or the opportunity to purchase branded merchandise. At times, fun interactive activities and creative challenges have been used to engage audiences in the action. Loads more information is posted here to satisfy fans' hunger for event details.

The Academy Museum posts ticket information once they become available to the public, and give hints to what is in store for each special event. The museum has a full calendar of events that are not related to Oscar Week, but its great to know the exhibits and other activities you can take advantage of while you're there.

*See TCM's 31 Days of Oscar*

Binge watch Oscar-nominated films for 31 days straight on Turner Classic Movies. The television program, which has been running since 1995, shows a select number of movies, varying in genre and release date, that are broadcast continually, all day and all night. Know that the word "classic" doesn't necessarily mean ancient. Yes, the program includes older films from the '30s, but it also includes some from the early 2000s and a lot of other movies made between those decades. Typically, TCM has a theme for each year, and a PDF of the program schedule is available on the TCM website, which allows you to plan your viewing sessions accordingly.

*Explore Oscars.org*

If reading books is not your thing and you're more a consumer of digital content, then go to the Academy of Motion Picture Arts and Sciences website to learn about the organization and the history of the Oscars. Click on Awards to learn about the other awards programs and their rules and eligibility. Click on Learn to read about the programs available to independent filmmakers. Click on News to see the Academy's digital magazine called A Frame and to read recent media releases..

*Check out the Oscars on YouTube*

Of all of the content that is posted on YouTube, hone in on Academy Conversations. Look for videos that feature nominees for the forthcoming Oscar awards. Most of what you'll find are Q&A sessions discussing films that have been nominated for the more popular categories, such as best picture, best director, best actor, and best actress. It's fascinating to hear the inside scoop about the film's development from the directors, producers, actors, and other cast and crew. It truly enriches your film experience.

*Follow Oscar Pundits*

In addition to following the Academy on social media, there are others pushing out content consistently during Oscar season. In no particular order, check out these outlets on social media platforms: The Hollywood Reporter, The LA Times' "The Envelope," The New York Times' "The Projectionist. People magazine, Entertainment Weekly magazine, and Sasha Stone @AwardsDaily.

# PART II:
# A.M.P.A.S.

# CHAPTER 4 -

## The Organization

Although the Academy of Motion Picture Arts and Sciences has been in existence for nearly a century, it has a certain mystique. This humongous members-only club emanates exclusivity, thus elevating Oscar fans' curiosity. Its brand exudes class, elegance, and stature, and in spite of its reputation as an old, white men's club, it upholds strict artistic standards, thus making it the world's preeminent movie-related organization.

# THE ACADEMY OF MOTION PICTURE ARTS AND SCIENCES

## AMPAS

The Academy of Motion Picture Arts and Sciences (AMPAS) is a nonprofit organization made up of film industry experts, including actors, special effects professionals, and more. Founded in 1927, the organization has maintained its focus on film excellence while organically evolving its breadth and scope. As of 2023, its membership exceeds 10,000, and it employs approximately 700 people. Its headquarters is in Beverly Hills. AMPAS also has two resource libraries located in another locations within Los Angeles: the Margaret Herrick Library at the Fairbanks Center for Motion Picture Study in Beverly Hills, and the Pickford Center for Motion Picture Study in Hollywood. In addition, AMPAS has two theaters available for rent: the Samuel Goldwyn Theater inside its home office in Beverly Hills and the Linnwood Dunn Theater located inside the Pickford Center for Motion Picture Study in Hollywood. Its largest facility is the Academy Museum of Motion Pictures, a six-story building that showcases film history, interactive exhibits, and a real Oscar statuette that fans can behold.

The organization, which uses several names, The Academy, The Academy Award(s), AMPAS, and Oscar(s), seeks to recognize and uphold excellence in the motion picture arts and sciences, inspire imagination, and connect the world through the medium of motion pictures. In addition to the Oscar ceremony, it has public programs ranging from screenings with panel discussions to summer intern programs to spark creativity, bolster education, and support emerging industry talent. A lot of time and money goes into running this organization. According to its June 2022 consolidated financial statement, it had $1,363,593,000$ in assets and $519,139,400 in liabilities.

The Academy's staff is led by an executive team responsible for daily operations. This executive team, referred to as the administration, consists of the chief executive officer, chief financial officer, chief communications officer, chief technology officer, chief operating officer, chief legal officer, chief membership, impact and industry officer and the chief of staff to the CEO and president and the chief audience officer for the Academy Museum are also on AMPAS's executive team.

## Branches

AMPAS members, led by the Board of Governors, are divided into 18 branches, representing the different facets of filmmaking:

Actors
Casting Directors
Cinematographers
Costume Designers
Directors
Documentary
Executives

Film Editors
Makeup Artists and Hairstylists
Marketing & Public Relations
Music
Producers
Production Design
Production and Technology Branch
Short Film and Feature Animation
Sound
Visual Effects
Writers

## Membership

To become an AMPAS member, you must work in the industry and be involved with theatrically released films. There are two avenues to entry: be recommended by an Academy member or be an Oscar nominee. When being referred, the first requirement is to be sponsored by two Academy members in your respective branch. The second requirement is that you meet the eligibility criteria established by that branch. The initial process is different for individuals who have been nominated for an Academy Award; they're automatically considered for membership. In both cases, the executive committee from the appropriate branch reviews prospective members' credentials. Then the Board of Governors determines who is worthy of an invitation to join. The new membership drive happens once a year, typically in the spring, weeks after the Academy Awards ceremony.

All members are required to maintain a high ethical standard to align with the Academy's mission of excellence and to foster an inclusive and creative environment. The organization has standards of conduct, and it expects members to demonstrate positive behavior to uphold these principles and to report violations when witnessed. AMPAS does not tolerate members abusing their status, influence, or professional power to discriminate, harass, or abuse. Members who demonstrate such behavior are suspended or expelled.

## Board of Governors

The Board of Governors is a leadership group made up of AMPAS members, each serving up to two three-year terms. Each governor is an executive committee member of their respective branch, and each branch has three governors serving on the board. The Board of Governors is responsible for ensuring that the organization's mission is fulfilled, that its finances are secure, and that it has a strategy for the future.

The Board of Governors votes for its leadership members in the summer, and the executive team begins its term in the upcoming fiscal year. The board is led by the following positions:

### Officers

One President
Six Vice Presidents
One Vice President/ Treasurer
One Vice President/ Secretary
CEO of AMPAS

Officers serve a one-year term and may serve up to four years in any one office. Each officer also is a chair for other committees. Committees within the organization are:

### Committees
Awards and Events
Museum
Preservation and History
Education and Outreach
Finance
Membership and Administration
Inclusion Advisory Committee

AMPAS also has a Science and Technology Council, which is tasked with resolving and researching issues in the industry, capturing the history and use of motion picture science and technology, and educating industry professionals and the public about technological contributions to film art.

## The Academy Foundation

AMPAS recognized the importance of education, culture, and film archives early in its development as an organization and established the Academy Foundation in 1944 as a separate nonprofit entity. At that time, its charge was to support film research and lead educational and cultural activities for AMPAS. The Academy had already been involved in supporting collegiate education since the 1920s and had assisted the Library of Congress with paper prints of films produced from the late 1800s to early

1900s. The Foundation uses the monetary gifts and donations it receives—such as funding from corporations and money given by individuals—to administer the Academy's educational, cultural, and film archival activities.

# FACILITIES FOR THE PUBLIC

## The Academy Museum of Motion Pictures

When this facility opened in 2021, it became the largest movie museum in the world. The Academy transformed a 1939 historical building, previously occupied by the Wilshire May Company department store, and added space to create a one-of-a-kind museum that showcases motion picture art and science in educational, experiential, and entertaining ways. This project launched in October 2012, after being approved by the Board of Governors. Shortly thereafter, a capital campaign was launched, led by Bob Iger, Annette Benning, and Tom Hanks, to raise funds to plan, design, and construct this 290,000 square foot complex.

The design by acclaimed architects Renzo Piano and Zoltan Pali distinguishes this museum from its neighbors on Museum Row in Los Angeles because the building's exterior has two elements that immediately catch your attention: the large ball with the glass dome roof and the gold cylinder. The ball, which looks suspended in air called "The Sphere," has a glass-covered top for the Dolby Family Terrace, giving visitors a stunning view of the

Hollywood Hills. The gold cylinder is located on the side of the original Wilshire May Company building, now called the Saban Building. It is a six-story structure that contains an educational studio, the Ted Mann theater, galleries, a store, and a cafe. The gold cylinder is made up of 350,000 one-inch square 24-karat gold glass mosaic tiles.

For cinephiles who want to know the juicy story behind the Academy Museum and why took almost a century to erect a movie museum in Los Angeles need to check out my book, Inside the Academy Museum: Elevate Your Visitor Experience from Memorable to Transformational.

## Fairbanks Center for Motion Picture Study

Having amassed a huge collection of movie-related documentation, such as scripts, movie posters, and photographs from 1928 onward, the Academy needed a large facility in which to store and share its collectibles. It outgrew the library space it had occupied, so it renovated the abandoned City of Beverly Hills Water Treatment Plant to serve as a storage center and library in 1991. It is named after AMPAS's first president, actor Douglas Fairbanks, because in 1927 he was a major proponent for the development of the water treatment plant. The Fairbanks Center contains the Margaret Herrick Library, named after the former AMPAS librarian and executive director, who worked for AMPAS for 40 years.

## Pickford Center for Motion Picture Study

Located in Hollywood, the Pickford Center contains the Academy Film Archive, a collection of films, Oscar telecasts, Academy Award-winning films, and special film collections. Named after Mary Pickford, an AMPAS founding member, silent screen actress, Oscar winner, and co-founder of United Artists, the Pickford Center contains films collected since 1929. The Academy Film Archive was established in 1991 and is available to researchers who need to view a film in its original form. In addition to storing and making films available to the public, the Film Archive has also actively preserved more than 1,100 films, and it digitizes and converses videotaped items. On occasion, films are screened in the Linnwood Dunn Theater, located inside.

# OTHER AWARD PROGRAMS

In addition to the Oscars, the Academy hosts several other film-related award programs to recognize excellence in motion picture arts and sciences. Most Oscar fans haven't heard of these award ceremonies because they are not as star-studded as the Academy Awards, and they focus more on contributions to the craft rather than on celebrity recognition and fashion. These private events do not occur during Oscar Week however, the event dates are announced to the public in advance and recaps are posted on AMPAS's social media.

## Governors Awards

This invitation-only, black-tie dinner occurs in November, when movie industry professionals—most of whom have achieved significant milestones in a lifelong career—are recognized for their work. Academy members can recommend honorees; however, the Board of Governors has sole authority to select winners. Selection typically occurs in September.

There are three different types of awards, though not every type is awarded every year.

### The Honorary Award

An Oscar statuette is given to an individual from any traditional discipline in the film industry who has performed exceptional work in their lifetime, or to an Academy member who has given outstanding service to the organization, or to a professional who has contributed greatly to the motion picture arts and sciences. Formerly known as the Special Award when inducted in 1929, some recipients are Charlie Chaplin, D.W. Griffith, Fred Astaire, Greta Garbo, Orson Welles, Sophia Loren, and Spike Lee.

### The Jean Hersholt Humanitarian Award

Periodically, an Oscar statuette is given to an individual in the motion picture industry whose humanitarian work has made a significant difference in the world. It's appropriately named after Jean Hersholt (1886–1956), a Danish American screen actor in the 1920s who led the

Motion Picture Relief Fund as president in the 1930s and '40s. The Motion Picture Relief Fund was an organization that offered financial support to actors and other movie professionals who were out of work or fell on hard times. Hersholt also served as AMPAS president from 1945 to 1949. Some award recipients since its 1957 induction include Bob Hope, Frank Sinatra, Audrey Hepburn, Quincy Jones, Jerry Lewis, Oprah Winfrey, and Angelina Jolie. 2021 has been the only year when the Board of Governors voted to amend the rules, and deemed an organization, Motion Picture & Television Fund (MPTF), as an award recipient, in addition to an individual, Tyler Perry.

*The Irving G. Thalberg Memorial Award*

Specifically recognizing producers whose work has been consistently exceptional and high quality, this award is not an Oscar statuette but rather a gold sculpture of Irving G. Thalberg's head. Thalberg helped form Metro-Goldwyn-Mayer and worked as head of production at age 26, in 1925. He set the standard for outstanding and elegant motion pictures, building a stellar reputation for MGM as an industry leader. This award is also gifted periodically. Some recipients since its 1938 induction are Walt Disney, Cecil B. DeMille, Alfred Hitchcock, Steven Spielberg, George Lucas, and Francis Ford Coppola.

## Sci-Tech Awards

AMPAS hosts the Academy's Scientific and Technical Awards at a formal affair in an elegant hotel in the Los

Angeles area to honor individuals and corporations that have significantly elevated the use of science and technology in filmmaking. Recognizing early on that science and technology are foundational to movie making, the Academy began acknowledging these industry professionals in 1931 at the 4th Academy Awards. There are three levels of awards: Academy Award of Merit (Class I) winners receive an Oscar statuette, Scientific and Engineering Award (Class II) winners receive a 24k gold-plated award tablet, and Technical Achievement Award (Class III) winners receive a certificate.

## John A. Bonner Medal of Commendation

Selected by the Scientific and Technical Awards Committee and the Academy Board of Governors, this honor is awarded to an Academy member who has demonstrated exceptional service and dedication to AMPAS. John A. Bonner, a sound engineer, was Director of Special Projects at Warner Hollywood Studios and had been awarded the Medal of Commendation in 1994. This award is presented at the Sci-Tech Awards ceremony.

## Gordon E. Sawyer Award

Given to an individual whose contributions brought credit to the motion picture industry, this honoree is also selected by the Scientific and Technical Awards Committee and the Academy Board of Governors. Named after three-time Oscar winner and former head of the sound department at Samuel Goldwyn Studios, Gordon E. Sawyer award winners receive an Oscar statuette. This award is presented at the Sci-Tech Awards ceremony.

## Student Academy Awards

Established in 1972, the Student Academy Awards is for full-time undergraduate and graduate students in the United States and abroad who have created a motion picture. Supported by the Academy Foundation, there is an open call in the spring for student filmmakers to submit their work, due typically in the summer. The awards ceremony, when winners receive medals, certificates, and prizes, typically takes place in October at the Samuel Goldwyn Theater. Domestic film categories include animation, documentary, narrative, and alternative. International film categories include animation, documentary, and narrative.

Proven to be an inspiration platform within the industry for filmmakers to showcase and advance their craft, past winners of the Student Academy Awards have gone on to earn 12 Oscars and 63 Oscar nominations. Academy Award winners include filmmakers John Lasseter, Spike Lee, and Robert Zemeckis.

## Academy Nicholl Fellowships in Screenwriting Awards

The Academy Nicholl Fellowships in Screenwriting competition is open to individuals and pairs who have written an original feature movie script. Supported by the Academy Foundation, it exists to boost fresh writing talent through a fellowship program in which up to five winners receive $35,000 each and are tasked with writing a new feature-length screenplay within a year. Winners spend a week in Los Angeles, participating in official awards week educational and social events. The awards ceremony, which typically occurs in November, is a public event, and a scene from the winners' screenplay is read aloud by prominent movie actors in front of a live audience.

Named after Don and Gee Nicholl, the first award program took place in 1986 to foster screenwriting talent. The Academy has an open call for entries in late winter, with a deadline of mid-spring. One of the best-known fellows is Susannah Grant, screenwriter for *Erin Brockovich* (2000) which earned her an Academy Award nomination and Ehren Kruger for co-writing *Top Gun: Maverick* (2022).

# AMPAS PROGRAMS AND PROJECTS

## Gold Rising

This program, formerly known as Academy Gold Talent and Development and Inclusion Program is an internship and mentoring program that began in 2017. The program offers college students and young professionals from underrepresented communities the opportunity to spend an eight-week stint in Los Angeles, working with industry professionals.

## Academy's Gold Network

There are other programs AMPAS offers young film professions in addition to Academy Gold, such as Gold Fellowship for Women designed for emerging women filmmakers; Gold Film Accelerator program for Latino filmmakers and the Jonas Gwangwa Music Composition Initiative designed for Black British musicians interested in composing music for film. Collectively, all of the programs make up the Academy's Gold Network and individuals who have successfully completed at least one of the main programs are eligible to be a part of the Gold Network, and are paired with an AMPAS member mentor through the Gold mentorship program. The fellowship combines direct financial support with personalized mentorship, access to once-in-a-lifetime networking opportunities, and lifelong career advancement support via the Gold Alumni Program.

## Careers in Film Summit

This free one-day event in Los Angeles is aimed at high school and college students from underrepresented backgrounds to inspire and give insight of jobs and a career path in the film industry. Taking place in May at the Academy Museum and streamed on YouTube, numerous Academy members give expert guidance and advice about the specific creative branch they belong to, and relay what its like being a professional in that trade.

## Academy Film Scholars Program

Supported by the Academy Foundation, the Academy Film Scholars supports new scholastic works and awards money to individual scholars, film festivals, and cultural organizations. The program was paused in 2022 due to budget adjustments resulting from the COVID pandemic, however be on the lookout for its resurgence.

## Oral History Program

The Academy has recorded in-depth interviews with many significant filmmakers. Transcriptions of those interviews are bound and available on-site at the Academy Film Archive through the Public Access Center. The Academy is dedicated to unifying and managing all forms of oral history at the Academy—recording, collecting, curating, and preserving.

## The Academy Visting Artists Program

As part of its public outreach, the Academy grants permission to academia, film festivals, industry conferences, and other film-related events, to have its members participate. Academy members visit students and faculty, creating a meaningful connection between the worlds of academia and practice at the industry's highest levels. The goal of the program is to connect institutions of higher learning with highly regarded professionals in the film industry.

# PART III:

# ULTIMATE EXPERIENCE FOR OSCAR FANS

# CHAPTER 5 -

## Oscar Tour

This chapter is your one-stop source for essential information on Oscar-related venues. Being that Los Angeles has been home to the Academy of Motion Picture Arts and Sciences since 1927, there are numerous places you can visit that are Oscar-related; however, the venues listed here can be considered the shining stars of AMPAS venues. This self-guided unofficial Oscar Tour will enrich your Oscar Week experience, and it will bring you closer to AMPAS' mission and vision for motion picture arts and sciences. Sites are grouped into "Places to Visit" and "Places to Stroll By," based on accessibility.

## PLACES TO VISIT

**Margaret Herrick Library**
**Fairbanks Center for Motion Picture Study**

*333 South La Cienega Boulevard*

The library is available to the public year-round and is primarily utilized by individuals studying, researching, or working on film projects. The library has a vast and exquisite collection of archived material, ranging from photographs to scripts. Established a year after the Academy was founded in 1927, it was named after Margaret Herrick in order to acknowledge her significant contributions as the Academy's librarian and executive director. Herrick was instrumental in establishing what is now known as one of the world's best film libraries.

This is a film geek's paradise. Those who want to wig out on all this goodness should plan on spending the entire day there. If you're just sort-of interested, plan a one-hour visit and determine in advance an item that you would enjoy seeing. For example, you can read the screenplay of a specific movie or see the poster or still shots from a movie. There are also books and artifacts on display, so you can walk around and read what's on the wall. An overview of the library's offerings can be found at www.oscars.org, by clicking Museum/Collection. The library has specific service dates and hours, so check their online schedule when planning your visit.

## The Hollywood Roosevelt Hotel

*7000 Hollywood Boulevard*

The Blossom Room inside the Hollywood Roosevelt Hotel served as the venue for the first Academy Awards on May 16, 1929, honoring outstanding films released between August 1, 1927, and August 1, 1928. The Blossom Room, which still exists, was an elegant space for the lavish dinner and ceremony in which industry professionals recognized their peers for exceptional performance.

## Biltmore Hotel

*506 South Grand Avenue*

The awards program took place at this luxury hotel in downtown Los Angeles irregularly between 1935 and 1943. Now named The Biltmore Los Angeles, the interior design remains quite grand and ornate, and there is an exhibit in the Historic Corridor with photographs and artifacts from the numerous Academy Award ceremonies that took place in the Sala D'Oro and Biltmore Bowl rooms.

## Fashion Institute of Design & Merchandising (FIDM)

*919 S. Grand Avenue*

Costumes from Academy Award nominated films in the Best Costume Design category are on display, in addition to costumes from other well-known movies. The Institute has a tradition of showcasing costume designs for Oscar-worthy films, allowing fans to see these life-giving works of textual art for free. Their exhibition, which is on display weeks before the Academy Awards ceremony, is typically populated with a variety of works, and a must-see, as it's the only one of its kind around the world.

## TCL Chinese Theatre

*6925 Hollywood Boulevard*

This famous theatre in the heart of Hollywood is one of the most beloved venues movie fans from all over the world recognize immediately. Most commonly known as the Grauman's Chinese Theatre, the Oscars took place here from 1944 to 1946, hosting the 16th, 17th, and 18th Academy Awards. The theatre, currently named TCL Chinese Theatre offers 30-minute tours of the building, seven days a week, except when closed for special events, such as film festivals, movie premieres, and award programs. Tour tickets are approximately $15 and can be purchased online.

## Dolby Theatre®

*6801 Hollywood Boulevard*

This venue is a definite sight to see, but it's a catch 22 if you plan to visit during Oscar Week. This venue, formerly the Kodak Theatre, is the current site for the Oscars, so it's partially inaccessible to patrons for days before the big night. Normally, you can walk around the perimeter for free or spend approximately $25 for a ticketed tour of the place, but it's a bust days before showtime. What you're missing out on is walking up the grand stairway graced with glass columns etched with best picture winners and the opportunity to have an expert guide take you inside the theatre and backstage. The upside to visiting during Oscar Week is seeing the assembly and production of this major world event in action. Although the chain-link fence that surrounds the place is somewhat prohibitive, you can clearly see all of the exterior visual elements, design, and decor coming together for Oscar night. The sidewalk directly in front of the theatre is blocked off, but you can see the action from across the street. Visit anytime before the big day because this area, along with neighboring streets, is completely closed off to vehicle and pedestrian traffic on the day of the awards.

## Hollywood Pantages Theatre

*6233 Hollywood Boulevard*

The only way to see the inside of this gorgeous historic venue is by purchasing a ticket to a live show playing there. It's worth it because the interior of this presentation palace is a time capsule of the 1930s. The walls are ornate, and the ceilings are embellished. You could stare at the inside of this joint for hours. Currently named Hollywood Pantages, this was home to the Oscars from 1950 to 1960.

# PLACES TO STROLL BY

## The Academy Film Archive
## Pickford Center for Motion Picture Study

*1313 Vine Street*

This facility contains the Academy's film collection, a treasure of more than 190,000 items that the organization has been collecting since 1929. Located in Hollywood, the archive is accessible only to film industry professionals or individuals with valid research aims, only by appointment, and only if the particular film in question is not available elsewhere. A 36-hour minimum advance notice is required for viewing appointments—the film needs at least 24 hours to air out, so to speak, and the staff needs time to physically inspect it beforehand. You can make a formal request online to gain in-person access to an archived item.

In addition to housing Academy Award-winning films and Oscar telecasts, it also has a large variety of individual collections, such as an Alfred Hitchcock collection, a Charles Guggenheim collection, and a Douglas Fairbanks, Jr., collection. Films are viewed onsite; there are no checkouts. Laptops, pen, and paper are allowed for taking notes, but recording devices and phones are prohibited.

The Linwood Dunn Theater, a 286-seat theater named after visual pioneer Linwood Dunn, is also located here. It is equipped to screen 16mm, 35mm, and 70mm films, as well as digital. The theater serves as a venue for lectures and Q&As as well as occasional Academy events.

## Dorothy Chandler Pavilion
## Los Angeles County Music Center

*135 North Grand Avenue*

This performance space is located across the street from the eye-catching Walt Disney Concert Hall, and it served as ceremonial space for the Academy Awards from 1969 to 1986, 1990 to 1994, 1996, and 1999. It's the only venue in Oscar history that served the Academy across four decades of award programs, beginning with the 41st Academy Awards in 1969 and ending with the 71st Academy Awards in 1999. Tours of the pavilion are not available, so the only way to see the inside is to purchase tickets to a live performance. However, it's worth the trip to see the exterior: Music Center Plaza, a beautiful courtyard with a spectacular water fountain.

# PART IV:
# THE BEST LAID PLAN

# CHAPTER 6 -

## Ideal Itinerary

Having given great care and attention to plan an Oscar Week trip, this itinerary is an ideal schedule for making the most of your time in Los Angeles during the days preceding the Academy Awards. Arrive in the city at least one day before the Oscar Week events start so that you experience the complete this Oscar Tour. This itinerary takes a lot of guesswork trying to figure out what to do first and where to go, so use it as a sure plan or as a mere suggestion list to make your trip outrageously awesome.

Since most of your afternoons will be spent at the Academy Museum of Motion Pictures, it is best to view Oscar-nominated films during the day and late evenings. A lot of international films are not widely distributed, so plan on seeing those while you're in town. If the weather forecast is sunny skies, plan a trip to see films in Santa Monica, where you can dip your toes in the sand of the Pacific Ocean or walk along the pier. Also, try to see a movie at one of the unique theaters during the day.

Plan to take the Oscar Tour (see Chapter 5). The venues listed below for Day One are in geographical order to keep you on a direct path versus steering you back and forth across town. Make it easy on yourself and rent a car or hire a ride-share service instead of taking public transportation. The schedule f covers a lot of ground, so taking public transportation on Day One may require you to break this agenda into two days.

The hours of operation for the sites listed here are subject to change, so double check the specific sites before you head out. Obviously, your transportation, lodging, meals, and souvenirs are at your expense. If there is a charge to enter the site, it is noted with a ($) in key code.

Key code:     (V) Places to visit
              (S) Places to stroll by
              ($) Cost for admission

# RECOMMENDED SCHEDULE

**Day One – Terrific Tuesday: Oscar Tour**
Arrive in Los Angeles

*DOWNTOWN L.A.*
Los Angeles Biltmore hotel (V)
*506 South Grand Avenue*

Dorothy Chandler Pavilion (S)
Los Angeles County Music Center
*135 North Grand Avenue*

Fashion Institute of Design & Merchandising (V)
*919 S. Grand Avenue*

*BEVERLY HILLS*
The Academy Museum of Motion Pictures (S)
*6067 Wilshire Boulevard*

Margaret Herrick Library (V)
Fairbanks Center for Motion Picture Study
*333 South La Cienega Boulevard*

12:30 p.m. Lunch

*HOLLYWOOD*
The Academy Film Archive (S)
Pickford Center for Motion Picture Study
*1313 Vine Street*

Dolby Theatre® (S)
*6801 Hollywood Boulevard*

TCL Chinese Theatre ($)(S)
*6925 Hollywood Boulevard*

The Hollywood Roosevelt Hotel (V)
*7000 Hollywood Boulevard*

Shop for souvenirs

Purchase The Hollywood Reporter Oscar edition

6:30 p.m. Dinner

Hollywood Pantages Theatre ($)(S)
*6233 Hollywood Boulevard*
(Purchase tickets for an evening performance in advance.)

Lodging check-in
5 p.m. Dinner
6 p.m. Samuel Goldwyn Theater doors open (V)
7 p.m. Short Films: Animated and Live Action event begins ($)

**Day Two – Wednesday**
8 a.m. Breakfast
10 a.m.  See nominated films at local cinemas
1 p.m. Panel of animated short film nominees
3 p.m. Animated short films screening (encore)

6 p.m. Panel of animated feature film nominees

9 p.m. See nominated films at local cinemas

## Day Three – Thursday

8 a.m. Breakfast

10 a.m. See nominated films at local cinemas

1 p.m. Panel of documentary short film nominees

3 p.m. Documentary short films screening (encore)

6 p.m. Panel of documentary feature film nominees

9 p.m. See nominated films at local cinemas

## Day Four – Friday

8 a.m. Breakfast

10 a.m. See nominated films at local cinemas

1 p.m. Panel of live action short film nominees

3 p.m. Live action short films screening (encore)

6 p.m. Panel of international feature film nominees

9 p.m. See nominated films at local cinemas

## Day Five – Saturday

8 a.m. Breakfast

10 a.m. See nominated films at local cinemas

1 p.m. Panel of makeup and hairstyling nominees

3 p.m. Exhibit of nominees' work

7 p.m. Last chance to see the Oscar setup outside the Dolby Theatre

## Day Six – Sensational Sunday: Oscars Night at the Museum

2:30 p.m. Arrive at the Academy Museum Prep for the big night

3 – 10 p.m. Walk the red carpet and enjoy all the offerings

## Day Seven – Magnificent Monday
Watch ABC-TV shows
>Good Morning America
>Live with Kelly and Mark

Depart Los Angeles with memories of an ultimate Oscar Week experience!

## CHAPTER 7 -

## Top 10 Tips

Now that you've come to the end of this guide, here is a summary of what you need to know when planning for this Oscar experience. All of this is possible, and you have all of the information to make this happen, so go for it.

### 1. Get a head start on planning your trip.

The Academy announces key dates during the summer, so you can begin planning several months in advance since you know Oscar Week happens the week preceding the Academy Awards ceremony. After you've marked your calendar for Oscar Week, then begin planning your flight, lodging, transportation, and daily adventures. Also mark your calendar for other important activities, like subscribing to The Hollywood Reporter, registering for

ABC TV morning shows, and purchasing Oscar Week tickets.

## 2. Arrive early to David Geffen Theater.

Parking is limited and so are the seats, so get there early. The doors open 30 minutes before showtime, so plan to be there at that time, so you can secure a great seat, take a few uncrowded photos, post social media updates, use the facilities, and settle in for an intriguing evening.

## 3. Plan on late nights.

If you opt for an early dinner so that you can get to the theater early, then you will be famished afterwards. Remember, no food is allowed inside the theater, only bottled water. The evening programs conclude between 7 and 7:30 p.m., so you can make a mad dash to a cinema to catch an Oscar-nominated film or visit a cocktail bar for a nightcap.

## 4. Spend daytime hours watching films.

For a complete Oscar Week experience, you'd have to see approximately 28 films, in those select categories, in approximately four weeks before this series of events begins. A few movies might be available online, so you can watch those before or as you travel to L.A., but a majority of the international films are not easily accessible. Take advantage of what the movie theaters in the Los Angeles area have to offer and see those films during the day while you're in town.

## 5. Secure paper souvenirs in a sturdy folder.

For those who dig keepsakes and souvenirs, take a heavy folder or envelope to keep your event wristband and other event materials intact. You can also use it to store your Oscar-themed magazines and movie postcards of nominated films available at some cinemas.

## 6. Spend at least one day in Santa Monica.

You'll be really close to the beach, and it's worth it to spend some time there. The good news is that there are movie theaters in the area, so you could see a flick in the morning, have lunch seaside, then head back to the museum in time an Oscar Week event. Remember to pack accordingly.

## 7. Create a trip playlist.

Use the power of music to encapsulate this exceptional experience by creating a personalized playlist specifically for this trip. Select an Oscar-nominated original song, pop hits, or whatever style of music you like that will remind you of this audacious adventure. Every time it's played, a rush of great memories will flood your brain with fulfillment and joy.

## 8. Eat at a Wolfgang Puck restaurant.

This celebrity chef has been catering Oscar events for years, and getting a taste of the high life is easy, being that he has a variety of restaurants in town. Review your options, select a place, make a reservation, then savor the flavors of a culinary experience you will always remember. Wolfgang Puck Catering also serves Oscars Night at the Museum, so attending that event includes that special culinary element.

## 9. Journey to Hollywood and Highland by Saturday night.

Although security around the Dolby Theatre® is extremely tight, pedestrian traffic is still flowing on the sidewalks until the night before the Oscars. It's best to stroll around the area during the day so that you can get good pictures of the event billboard and sections of the red carpet setup. If you go on the day of the Academy Awards (not recommended), you'll be standing behind a chain-link fence hundreds of yards away from all of the action and won't be able to see much.

## 10. Attend an Oscar viewing event.

You're in a privileged position being in Los Angeles on Oscar night, so take advantage of your proximity and attend a viewing event. Research ticket options online weeks in advance, then purchase with confidence knowing you'll be celebrating the night with other fans who enjoy the thrill of it all as much as you do. Oscars Night at the Museum is not the only viewing event in town, but it's certainly the best bang for your buck.

# About the Author

Photo by Danny Owen Kohutek

**Catherine R. Lester** is a diehard Oscar fan devoted to guiding others through an enriching Academy Awards experience. She's discovered the inside scoop about golden opportunities that most fans don't know exist. Having researched, studied, and validated riveting resources, most of which are public offerings from the Academy of Motion Picture Arts and Sciences, Catherine has created this step-by-step guide that takes readers through AMPAS's Oscar Week.

Catherine educates filmmakers and movie fans about the Academy Awards with the goal of getting them to the Oscars. Her four books are the only ones in existence that pave the way to the red carpet for everyday people. Having studied the Oscars for nearly three decades, she has in-depth knowledge that greatly benefits filmmakers and movie fans.

Her fan experience includes viewing every Academy Awards' best picture nominee since 1997 and attending the following Academy of Motion Picture Arts and Sciences public events: the grand opening of the Academy Museum of Motion Pictures, Oscar Night at the Museum, Oscar Red Carpet Fan Experience, Oscar Week, Oscar Concert, and Singin' in the Rain and Hollywood Costume in Los Angeles, and Oscar Roadtrip and Oscar Fan

Experience in Texas. She is also a founding supporter of the Academy Museum of Motion Pictures and the author of three other guides for Oscar Fans:

- Academy Awards Excitement: How To Do Oscar Night Right
- Explore Oscar Season: Chart a Path to the Academy Awards
- Inside the Academy Museum: Elevate Your Visitor Experience from Memorable to Transformational

She has a B.A. in Communications, and is a member of Women In Film (WIF Los Angeles) and the American Film Institute (AFI).

Website: www.crlesterauthor.com

Facebook: CRLesterAuthor

Twitter: @CLesterPR

Catherine Lester's YouTube channel. Fan Experience - Academy Awards playlist

---

Did you attend Oscar Week using tips from this book? Post on social media and tag @CRLesterAuthor on Facebook @CLesterPR on X .

# RESOURCES

Academy of Motion Picture Arts and Sciences
www.oscars.org

Academy Museum of Motion Pictures
https://www.academymuseum.org/

The Official Academy Awards Database
http://awardsdatabase.oscars.org/

Margaret Herrick Library
http://www.oscars.org/library

*"85 Years of the Oscar"* by Robert Osborne

The Hollywood Reporter
www.thr.com

ABC-TV's Oscars news and information
www.oscars.go.com

The LA Times' "The Envelope"
http://www.latimes.com/entertainment/envelope/

The New York Times' "The Carpet Bagger"
https://www.nytimes.com/column/the-carpetbagger

People magazine
http://people.com/

Entertainment Weekly
http://ew.com/

www.ingramcontent.com/pod-product-compliance
Lightning Source LLC
LaVergne TN
LVHW021411080426
835508LV00020B/2561